Photography for Kids

Photography
FOR KIDS
A Beginner's Book

LEARN HOW TO TAKE AMAZING PHOTOS

JP Pullos

ROCKRIDGE
PRESS

For Lydia, the source of creativity, self-expression, and pure, unbridled joy for tens of thousands of people, not least of all me.

For general information on our other products and services or to obtain technical support, please contact our Customer Care Department within the United States at (866) 744-2665, or outside the United States at (510) 253-0500.

Rockridge Press publishes its books in a variety of electronic and print formats. Some content that appears in print may not be available in electronic books, and vice versa.

TRADEMARKS: Rockridge Press and the Rockridge Press logo are trademarks or registered trademarks of Callisto Media Inc. and/or its affiliates, in the United States and other countries, and may not be used without written permission. All other trademarks are the property of their respective owners. Rockridge Press is not associated with any product or vendor mentioned in this book.

Interior and Cover Designer: Darren Samuel
Art Producer: Meg Baggott
Editor: Barbara J. Isenberg

Photography © Design Pics / Alamy, p xii; FotoHelin / Alamy, p. 24; Dream Lover / Stocksy United, p. 35; Tatyana Tomsickova / Alamy, p. 37; Milles Studio / Stocksy United, p. 65; Maria Altynbaeva / Stocksy United, p. 71; EyeEm / Alamy Stock Photo, p. 77; All other images used under license from iStock Photo and Shutterstock.com

Author photo courtesy of Lydia Billings

ISBN: Print 978-1-64739-769-2
eBook 978-1-64739-770-8
R1

Contents

Introduction

When I was growing up, I loved movies that were visually interesting and that told great stories, so I thought I might become a filmmaker. But when I was 10 years old, I picked up a film camera for the first time. I discovered that I loved being able to create images from my unique point of view. I enjoyed telling stories through my photography. Most importantly, taking pictures and showing them to others made me happy!

After that, I could not put my camera down. I was 21 years old when I moved to New York City to be a professional photographer. I carried my camera with me wherever I went. My friends started calling me a photographer even before I got my first photography job. It took me nine years to get hired as a professional photographer, and it was worth the wait. My first job was to take pictures of celebrities at movie premieres. It was thrilling to photograph actors I had seen in movies. I also got to take pictures at fancy charity events, at the opening of Broadway shows, and I even created images of some of my favorite musicians. My images were published in some of the biggest magazines, newspapers, and websites in the world. I was so proud. To this day, I really enjoy being a photographer.

That is why I am writing this book: I love teaching people how to share their creativity with others.

This book is special because the tips, tricks, and activities can be used by anyone, anywhere in the world, with any kind of camera. You can use digital cameras on smartphones and tablets, standalone digital cameras, and even film cameras. This book will give you the ability to be an artist with any device. You will learn to create stunning images that are uniquely yours.

Photographers have a certain way of looking at the world. We notice moments other people overlook. Photographers are great observers of what is going on around them. Photographers also have a special talent: they can anticipate the moments in life that will make a great image. Photographers are observant; they can sense that a magical moment is about to happen before it happens. Photographers are ready with their camera, so when the moment comes, they're ready to capture it.

In this book, you will learn to look at the world through a photographer's eyes, which means you will think about what you are about to create before you snap a photo. You will learn the art of taking fewer images that are each amazing, instead of taking a lot of "okay" pictures and maybe editing them. If you are a true beginner, you will be able to call yourself a photographer by the time you finish the activities in this book. If you already take pictures, you will expand your creative talents in a big way!

How to Use This Book

This book has two parts. Part 1 is a beginner's photography class that will teach you the basics of using a camera and the concepts behind taking a good photo. When you finish this part, you will have a solid understanding of how a camera works and how some of the most powerful functions work on a camera. Part 2 reviews those concepts with a series of fun activities that will turn you into a photographer. These activities were created so you become skilled at the various concepts and develop your creative voice.

This book uses several key features to guide you on your journey into photography. On the way, you will find:

» Glossary of camera/photography terms (see page 122): At various points in the book, I define camera and photography terms (for example, exposure, aperture, etc.). These are basic words that every serious photographer at any level needs to know. The important words will be in **bold** the first time they appear in the book and defined in the glossary at the back of the book for easy reference.

» Photo Tips: The Photo Tip boxes explain the technical details of great photos and show you ways to make adjustments in various real-life situations for best results.

» Arrows and callouts to examine sample photos: These make the techniques you are learning about clear to understand.

PART ONE

Beginner's Photography Class

CHAPTER ONE

Camera and Photo Basics

What Is Photography?

Cameras come in all shapes and sizes, but one thing is true of them all: cameras capture light. When you take a picture, you are documenting the light in the scene you are photographing. Whenever you create a photo, it is like you are painting with light. Cameras create photographs, and each photograph documents a moment in time. Because no two moments in time are the same, no two photographs are the same!

Starting all the way back in the 1800s, photography has been a critical and important part of cultures around the world. Photographs have been used to tell news stories, to advertise products, to capture the most special moments of people's lives, to bring attention to humanitarian issues, and to create art that people love to hang on their walls, among many other uses.

Most cameras people use today are digital cameras, but, for most of the history of photography, cameras used film instead of hardware and software to create images. In some ways, the change from film cameras to digital cameras was a big one, but, during and after that change, photography continued to be just as important as it always was.

For many generations, photography has been a fun hobby for some people and a fulfilling career for others. One of the great things about photography is that you can take excellent photos no matter what kind of camera you are using and no matter how much knowledge you have about photography!

History of Photography

Before photography was invented, artists used a device called a *camera obscura* to project a scene onto a piece of paper—upside-down—so they could draw or trace that scene onto the paper. In the 1820s, there were several people, in different places in the world, attempting to turn this process into a way of capturing a scene in a more precise way than a drawing. They did not have a word for it yet, but they were on the path to creating the first photograph! The very first photographic image ever created used a type of asphalt, which changes color when exposed to light. In the 1820s, inventors found a way to stop the color-changing process so that a picture could be created and saved over time.

Both asphalt and silver, which also changes color when exposed to light, were used for early images. But inventors wanted to find a way to make photography work on paper, to make it easier for more people to do, and, by 1839, they did it!

At first, photography became popular because of three kinds of **subjects**: people, landscapes, and architecture. People were amazed they could look at something on a piece of paper that was not drawn or painted that looked very much like reality.

Even though photography was invented in the 1820s, it was not until the 1880s, when George Eastman invented the Kodak #1 camera, that cameras were available in stores for everyday people to buy at a reasonable price. By 1900, the most popular camera for early hobbyists was the Kodak Brownie. Over many decades, millions of Brownie cameras were sold to people around the world.

When photography first became popular, there was debate among artists about whether photography should be considered "artistic." Some painters argued there was no creativity involved in pointing a camera and pressing a button. Photographers responded by arguing that they need a lot of artistic talent to create a beautiful image. Eventually, photographers won the debate, and photography is now considered an art form.

All photographic images created in the early days were black-and-white images. Inventors wanted to find a way to capture images with color—but it took them a long time to do so. The first color image taken was created in 1861. The process, however, was complicated and only people with specialized equipment could create images with color in them. It was not until 1935 that Kodak—the same company that made the Brownie camera—created and introduced color film for hobbyist and professional photographers to use.

For a long time, "photography" referred only to cameras that used film. In 1957, inventors started working on creating a camera that, instead of using film, would use components from a computer to create a digital image. Just like with color images, digital photography also took a long time to get into the hands of everyday photographers. It was not until the 1990s that digital cameras became widely available. Cellular phones and computers with built-in digital cameras became available in the early 2000s. Today, most cameras sold in the world are digital.

How a Camera Works

Cameras come in all shapes and sizes. A camera on a smartphone looks different from a large camera you might see being used at a sporting event. No matter the size of the camera, all cameras work the same. If you open a film camera and a digital camera, the insides will look very much alike.

Imagine you are taking a picture of a person. You can see that person because light is bouncing off the person and into your eyes. When you take a picture, that same light goes into the camera. Inside digital cameras, there is something called an **image sensor**, which is a flat rectangular piece of hardware that can read light and turn that light into a digital image file. If you are using a film camera, instead of an image sensor, you will have film inside the camera. Film changes color when it is exposed to light and can be used to create physical prints of your pictures.

There are several things in your camera that let in more light or less light. When less light is allowed into the camera, the photographed image will appear darker; when more light is let in, the photographed image will appear brighter.

The **camera body** is, on a standard camera, the main and biggest part of the camera, not including the lens.

The **lens** is the cylinder on the front of the camera. On some cameras, you can replace the lens with another lens, but with many others, you cannot.

The **viewfinder**, on cameras that have one, is the opening in the camera you look through to see the scene you are going to photograph before you take the picture.

Digital images are made up of **pixels**, which are tiny squares of color that combine to form a picture. Each pixel is only one color.

Zoom is a camera function that, when changed, makes it look like you are closer to or farther from your subject and allows you to include more or less of the scene in the final picture.

The **focus** on a camera refers to the objects that are clear instead of blurry in your photograph. You can focus on one object or you can have all the elements in your scene be in focus.

Exposure is how bright or dark an image is. Exposure is determined by how much light is in your scene, the aperture, shutter speed, and the ISO.

The **aperture** is an opening in a lens that gets smaller or bigger. The aperture acts like the pupil in your eye and lets in more light or less light, depending on the size of the opening.

The **shutter speed** dictates how long the light is let into a camera when you take a picture. This is controlled by the shutter, which opens for a certain amount of time.

The **ISO setting** indicates how sensitive the camera is to light. Just like some people are more sensitive or less sensitive to getting burned by the sun, your camera can be more or less sensitive to light.

Taking Care of Your Camera

No matter what type of camera you have, it is important to treat it carefully. Most cameras are made to take normal wear and tear, but cameras have a lot of small, sensitive pieces inside. Dropping your camera even once can result in damage beyond repair. You can, for example, scratch the glass on your lens. The camera would still work, but all your pictures might come out looking not quite the way you want them to. Taking proper care of your camera will ensure that it lasts for a long time and takes the best photos possible.

» When you are not using your camera, it is best to store it in a dry environment, so the camera does not get wet accidentally.

» You can buy protective camera cases for almost all cameras. These are useful to have so that, in case you drop the camera, it is less likely to be damaged.

» Before you take the camera out in the rain or snow, have a parent or other adult confirm that the camera is 100 percent waterproof. If it is not, do not get it wet.

» Keep the lens clean by using a mild cleaner and a soft, clean cloth. You can also ask a parent or other adult to buy some single-use lens-cleaning packets.

» Never touch anything on the inside of your camera, as you may break it.

» If there is a strap on your camera, use it! You can even buy straps for smartphones. This will make it less likely that you will drop the camera and damage it.

Thinking Like a Photographer

Photographers are perhaps the most observant people in the world. Great photographers are always attuned to everything happening around them. They are always thinking, "How can I create a great image in this environment?" Photographers also anticipate those magical moments that happen in life that, when captured, create stunning images. They not only anticipate those moments but are also ready to take the picture when it happens. After a moment has passed, have you ever thought to yourself, "That would have made a great picture"? Great photographers practice being ready for those moments, so they never miss them.

» You cannot be ready to take a picture if you do not have your camera with you. Always carry your camera with you. You will give yourself more opportunities to practice.

» Always be looking for subjects. Your subjects can be people, animals, landscapes, cars, buildings, or whatever you like. Remember, however, *do not take photos of people without their permission.*

» Great images always tell a story! This means that when someone looks at your image, they will enjoy how the image appears, and they will enjoy the story being told by the photo.

» Think about how images can work well together. Sometimes, to tell a story, you might need more than one image. Imagine three portraits next to one another of a grandma, a mom, and a daughter.

» Until you find what you really love to photograph, take pictures of everything around you. You might be surprised by what you end up discovering about yourself and your photography.

COLOR

We do not immediately think about color, because our eye focuses on the subject of the image. Colors in an image can be *muted*, which means they are not very bright. They can also be saturated. Saturated colors look very bright and vivid and really pop in an image. Colors can be complementary—like a shirt and pants that "go together"—or they can clash. Both are interesting to look at. Another technique for using color is to find a scene made up of very muted colors, except for one brightly colored object that stands out. This is a great way of having one big pop of color in your image!

What Makes a Good Photo?

There are five concepts that are the most important ones to know for creating a stunning image: framing, composition, lighting, depth and dimension, and lines. We will cover these ideas a lot more in part 2 of this book. If you want to be able to tell a good photo from a bad one, start by asking yourself, "Was the photographer thoughtful about these five things?" Remember, however, that these guidelines are meant to be broken from time to time. Sometimes, you will like an image that does not fit any of the concepts—and that is okay! These guidelines are appropriate for any kind of camera, whether you are using a smartphone camera or a standard camera. It will help you to familiarize yourself with them first and to understand how they work together.

Framing

Usually, when we think of the word "frame," we think of a frame you might buy for a painting or a picture. **Framing** also describes the creative process that goes into choosing a variety of things about every picture you take while you take it. Imagine you are taking a picture of a friend in a park. Do you stand close to your friend or farther away? Do you include a small part of the **background** or a lot of the background? Do you put your friend in the center of the image or off to the side? Do you zoom in or out? All these questions refer to what we call framing.

Composition

Composition is like framing and shares some of the same ideas but, in some ways, the two are different. Composition is how you arrange the elements inside your image, such as the subject and background, what **angle** you capture, and how close you are to the subject. Composition also refers to the **shapes** and **lines** in your image and how all the visual pieces work together. Imagine you took one image of a Ferris wheel with lots of people in your image. Next, imagine you took a close-up picture of the keys on a piano. Now imagine those two images next to each other. Can you see how the composition in each will be different?

Lighting

When you take a photograph, it is like you are painting with light. Every single image involves light of some kind. Without light, you cannot create a picture. The concept of **lighting** refers to how your subject is lit. Is your subject lit by sunlight from above? Is it lit by a lamp off to one side? Or is your subject in the shade? Each of these types of light will create a distinct look. You can change the lighting on your subject either by moving your subject, if possible, or taking the picture at another time of day, when the sun and clouds in your scene might look different. Most cameras have a flash, which will change the lighting as well.

Depth and Dimension

You likely have seen images that look flat (lifeless) and some that look like they have a three-dimensional quality to them. Images that look like they could be three-dimensional have **depth**, meaning you can sense the distance between the objects. The best landscapes have the element of depth. When you look at an image with depth, you can imagine standing where the camera is and walking into the scene in the picture. **Dimension** refers to an image having interesting elements in the **foreground**, **middle ground**, and background. In many images, just one of those three areas is interesting, but a photograph with dimension really takes advantage of all three at once. Images with dimension are often more dynamic and interesting.

Lines

Lines show up in images in many ways. Sometimes they are obvious. In a picture of the ocean and sky, the horizon (where the ocean meets the sky) is a very strong line. In a picture of a long road stretching out into the distance, the two lines on either side of the road will show up prominently. Lines can guide the viewers' eyes from one part of an image to another. Lines can be straight and horizontal (going from left to right), straight and vertical (going from top to bottom), or straight and diagonal (going from one corner to another). But lines are not always straight. Often, they are curved. Curved lines can be fun to see in an image!

CONTRAST

Each image has lighter parts and darker parts. **Contrast** refers to the difference between the lightest and darkest parts of the image. A photo with high contrast has a lot of difference between the light and dark areas of the image. This is particularly striking in black-and-white images, but contrast can make images with color really pop, too! Images with more contrast tend to look more professional, but contrast can be hard to create with just a camera. If you can **edit** an image (which means to alter the image after it was taken), then you should find out how to increase the contrast of your image. Try it and see if you like the result.

Safety and Manners: What Every Photographer Must Know

Before getting started, here are some dos and don'ts all young photographers must know:

DO

» Avoid dangerous spaces, like streets, edges near cliffs, pools, and all unsafe areas.

» Ask for help if you are not sure about safety.

» If your camera has a wrist or neck strap, always use it.

» If your camera or smartphone has a protective case, use it.

» Be aware of your surroundings at all times.

» If you are borrowing someone else's camera, ask permission before using it.

» Ask a parent or other adult what safety advice they have for you.

» Check the weather for possible rain or snow before you go out to see if you need to bring items such as an umbrella or a waterproof case to keep your camera dry.

DON'T

» Drop your camera.

» Set up your camera somewhere unsteady.

» Take pictures in places where you can trip or fall.

» Climb up high without adult supervision.

» Place yourself, people, objects, or your camera in unsafe places, like someplace high or near streets.

» Ask anyone to do anything in a picture they are uncomfortable doing.

» Use sharp objects without an adult's supervision.

» Approach strangers without an adult present.

» Take pictures of other people without asking permission first.

» Take candid photos of strangers.

» Get your camera or smartphone wet unless you have a waterproof camera.

» Block emergency exits.

» Use someone's belongings without their permission.

» Take and share photos that may embarrass someone, including on social media.

» Post any images on social media without permission from a parent or other adult.

» Store the camera with the lens off.

Getting Started: Photographer Checklist

This easy-to-use checklist summarizes everything you have learned so far! You can review this before you begin to set yourself up for staying safe and taking the best photos possible. Keep this list in mind, and refer to it, before you begin the activities in part 2.

○ Safety first: Always remember to think about your surroundings. Make sure you, your subjects, and your belongings are not in danger.

○ Are you wearing the wrist or neck strap if your camera has one?

○ Do you have your smartphone or camera in a protective case if it has one?

○ Did you check the weather to see about possible rain or snow? Did you bring everything you need to keep your camera dry?

○ Did you stage your subject and position yourself in a way that is safe?

○ Did you get the support of a parent or other adult if you need it to ensure you are completely safe?

○ Did you ask permission before taking your picture?

○ Have you looked at all four corners of your frame to make sure the composition looks exactly the way you want it?

○ Have you chosen the right distance between yourself and your subject?

- If your camera can zoom in and out, have you chosen a good zoom setting?

- Are you photographing from the best angle to capture your subject in the best way? Does the angle depict the shape and form of the subject?

- Are you creatively including any space around your subject, like the sky or a colorful wall?

- If you can move your subject, have you moved it to the best possible place?

- Before you take a picture, have you looked at the foreground, middle ground, and background to make sure all three look the way you want them to?

- Are you taking a picture that highlights objects that are both close to you and far away from you in the scene?

- Before you start composing your next image, have you assessed the light in the scene? Is there a lot of light (for example, sunlight) or is it a low-light scene (such as indoors or at night)?

- Is it a scene that would best be captured by natural light instead of using a flash? Would using your flash contribute anything to the image?

○ Are there a lot of shadows in your scene that you can creatively include?

○ Are you able to come back to the scene you are photographing at a different time of day to capture better light for optimal depth and dimension?

○ Before you take a picture, are you actively looking at the scene to see what lines you can identify and highlight in your subject to add depth and guide the viewers' eyes?

○ Have you identified the strong horizontal, vertical, diagonal, and/or curved lines in your scene?

CAREERS IN PHOTOGRAPHY

Professional photographers take pictures of all kinds of people and things. Photographs are used to advertise products and services; to demonstrate how to do things, such as put a toy together or cook a meal; and to make viewers aware of other cultures, the natural world, and so on. Here is a list of some of the possible careers you can think about pursuing when you are ready:

Advertising photography: creating photographs that are used to sell things, like toys and furniture

Artistic photography: creating photographs that are presented as works of art, usually in a gallery or museum

Automobile photography: creating pictures used to sell automobiles, or that display design and technological aspects of the vehicles

Editorial photography: creating images that appear in magazines, newspapers, and on websites to illustrate the articles

Fashion photography: creating photographs to display clothing design and sell clothes

Food photography: creating photographs to show the process and end product of cooking and baking

Humanitarian photography: creating images about struggles in the world to make a positive difference in the lives of the people affected

Nature and wildlife photography: creating photographs that teach about and appreciate nature

Photojournalism: telling a news story primarily through pictures and images

Portrait photography: creating portraits of celebrities, actors, businesspeople, students, families, and pets

Real estate photography: creating pictures used to sell or showcase homes and other buildings

Travel photography: creating photographs that encourage travel by showing great destinations

Wedding photography: creating a beautiful record of the start of a marriage

PART TWO

Becoming a Photographer

CHAPTER TWO
Framing

There are a lot of creative choices to make with each image you take. **Framing** is a collection of fun photography concepts. Once you learn these concepts, your ability to create amazing images will expand in a big way.

There are many different aspects to framing. You can think about just one aspect, or you can think about many aspects for whatever image you are taking. Imagine helping an adult make some cookies. You want to take pictures of what you made. You place some cookies on a plate. When you take the first picture, will you stand close to or far away from the cookies? Will you include the kitchen in the background or just the plate of cookies in the image? Will you photograph holding your camera horizontally (left to right) or vertically (up and down)? Will you take the picture standing above the cookies? Or will you position yourself so you are looking at them straight on? You can apply these questions to any photograph you take, whether it is of a person, a building, a landscape, or something else!

Subject

The subject is the most important element of your image. In a portrait, the person is the subject. If you take a picture of a beautiful sunset, there might also be a building in the image, but the subject is the sunset, not the building. You might have a lot of objects in your image; your subject is where you want whoever is looking at your image to focus their attention. For a picture of a lake, a mountain, and some trees, in which each element is equally important, you could say the entire scene is the subject.

Staging

Imagine you are at a birthday party. If you've already asked permission to take pictures of your friends, then you can take pictures of them while they're not paying attention or posing for the camera. This is called a **candid** photo. Now, imagine telling your friends, "Stand here. I am going to take your picture now." This is called **staging**. You can stage people or objects. If you are taking a picture of a plate of food, for example, you might want to stage the food, or arrange it on the plate, so it looks beautiful. In this chapter, you will learn how to think about all these things so you can snap the best pictures.

Orientation: Horizontal or Vertical

Unless you are using a camera that only takes perfectly square photographs, you have a choice of orientation every time you take a picture! Your choice is to photograph either horizontally or vertically. *Horizontally* means you are holding the camera with the long side of the camera extending left and right, so your image is framed extended left to right. *Vertically* means you are holding the camera with the long side of the camera extending up and down, so your image is framed extending up and down. There is no right or wrong choice between these two options. As a photographer, you get to choose which orientation you want to use for every picture you take. You will want to think this through before each one!

Perspective

Perspective refers to where you are in relation to your subject. In most pictures you see, the photographer is at eye level with the subject. This means the photographer was not positioned above or below the subject being photographed. They were on the same level. You can also take a picture from down low looking up at your subject, or from above your subject looking down at it. Perspective also refers to which side of your subject you are photographing. If you take a picture of a car, are you facing the front, back, or right or left sides of the car? Each perspective will look different and will have a different background as well!

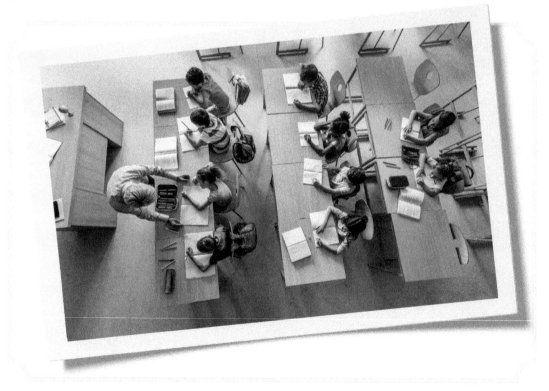

Natural Frames

A natural frame is any object in your scene that frames your subject. Imagine taking a picture of a friend standing in an open doorway. You can see that the doorframe will frame your friend in the image. Imagine you are inside a home and you can see a landscape out the window. You take a picture and include the window frame in the image. The landscape will be framed by the window frame. Practice looking for objects around you that will frame your subject. If you look hard enough, you will notice they are all around you.

PICTURE IT!

Vertical and Horizontal Framing

The goal of this activity is to practice choosing which orientation is best for each picture you take. Should you hold your camera vertically or horizontally? You will learn that this choice has a big impact on how your image looks and feels. You might find you prefer one over the other!

WHAT YOU'LL NEED

» A place to walk where you will see a few homes or buildings

» Dice

Steps

1. Ask a parent or other adult to walk with you.
2. Stand in front of the first home or building you come to. Roll the dice.
3. If an even number comes up, take a picture of the home or building horizontally. If an odd number comes up, take a picture of the home or building vertically.
4. Repeat the exercise with at least two more homes or buildings. You can do this with as many homes as you want!

PHOTO TIP

You have probably noticed that some social media apps display images as squares, which photographers call a *square aspect ratio*. Some cameras allow you to set a square aspect ratio before you take an image, but smartphones allow you to crop the image into a square after you have taken it. For standard cameras, you will need to use a computer to crop an image.

PHOTO LOG

Which orientation do you prefer, horizontal or vertical? Why?

....

....

....

Why do you think horizontal or vertical was better for the homes or buildings you photographed?

....

....

....

PICTURE IT!

Natural Frames

The goal of this activity is for you to start to see more than just the subject of your photograph. Including a natural frame in your picture adds a very interesting element for your viewer. It also forces you, as the photographer, to look at your entire scene!

WHAT YOU'LL NEED

» An indoor space with doorways and windows

Steps

1. Take 10 pictures standing in various places in your indoor space.
2. For each picture, use a doorway or a window as a natural frame in the image.
3. Your subject should be a variety of objects in your indoor space, or objects that are outside your space but visible through the windows. Use the doors and windows to frame the objects.

PHOTO TIP: Silhouette

In a **silhouette**, the subject is so dark that it looks completely black, but the rest of the scene is visible behind the subject. This can be accomplished by positioning your subject in front of a brighter background. For example, imagine you are inside a home and the sun is shining. You can open the door, tell a friend to stand inside the door, then, from inside, take a picture that includes your friend and the outside. In the resulting image, you will only be able to see the shape of your friend, not the details of their appearance. You can have fun with this by having your friend do different poses in the doorway.

PHOTO LOG

Do you think the natural frames made your images more interesting? Why or why not?

....

....

....

Which do you think makes a better natural frame—doors or windows? Why?

....

....

....

PICTURE IT!

Perspective

The goal of this activity is to learn that you have many different choices for what perspective to choose when you take a picture. You will learn to think about perspective before you snap every photo.

WHAT YOU'LL NEED

>> Any location, indoors or outdoors, that is fun or pretty

Steps

1. Pick a location (your home, your yard, a park, or anywhere interesting).
2. Take at least 15 pictures from the perspective, or point of view, of a small dog—close to the ground.
3. Switch to taking pictures from the perspective of a giraffe. Walk around on your tiptoes while taking pictures of the same scene. Take at least 15 pictures.
4. Switch to taking pictures from the perspective of how you would see your environment normally. Take at least 15 pictures from your eye level.

📷 PHOTO TIP

To get a high perspective, try holding your camera up high, even if you cannot see what you are about to photograph. This takes practice but will come in handy if you find yourself in a crowd and want to take a picture but cannot see in front of you. Be careful to choose a safe space to do this, where you are unlikely to fall or drop your camera. Remember, safety is the first rule in photography.

PHOTO LOG

Which perspective came out best? Why do you think so?

....

....

....

When you photographed at eye level, did you find yourself wanting to
get more creative after trying out the different perspectives? Why do you
think that is?

....

....

....

PICTURE IT!

Fill the Frame

The goal of this activity is to see that you can get really creative with how you frame your subjects, including getting close. Most photographs of one object have the object in the center of the image with space around it. That's not bad, but it's also not very creative.

WHAT YOU'LL NEED

>> 1 piece of fruit

>> A parent or other adult to cut the fruit

>> 1 flower or toy

Steps

1. Ask an adult to help you cut your piece of fruit in half.

2. Take a picture of the inside of the piece of fruit, so the fruit fills the entire frame and you can't see anything else.

3. Take 10 more photos of the fruit, trying different angles. See which ones come out the best.

4. Now pick a different subject, such as a flower or a toy, and take more photos in which the subject fills the frame.

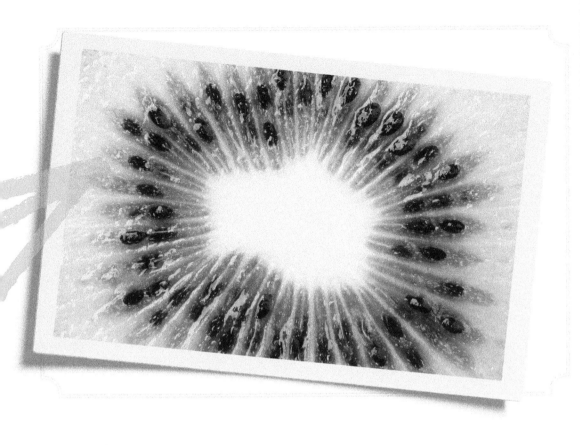

PHOTO LOG

Which object did you enjoy filling the frame with most? Why?

....

....

....

How was filling the frame with the fruit different from your second subject?

....

....

....

PICTURE IT!

Backgrounds

The goal of this activity is to learn to pay attention to what is behind your subject in addition to your subject. You will learn that it is wise to choose a background that complements your subject but does not distract from it.

>> A toy

>> A location, inside and/or outside, with different backgrounds to choose from (this can include walls with different colors or different pieces of furniture that are different colors)

Steps

1. Working with one background at a time, place the toy in front of 10 different backgrounds and take a picture of the toy that includes the background in each image.

2. Each background should be as different as possible from the others.

3. You can choose to include a small amount or a large amount of the background in each image.

📷 PHOTO TIP: Negative Space

When the background of a photograph is interesting, we might look at that as well. Sometimes there are spaces in an image where there's nothing to see, which can add a great visual element to the image. We call this negative space. Think about an image of plain blue sky with a small row of trees taking up the bottom part of the image. Your eyes will first look at the trees, but the visual statement of the image is unique because of all the negative space!

PHOTO LOG

Which background did you like best and why?

....

....

....

How much does it change the look and feel of an image by choosing a
different background for each?

....

....

....

PICTURE IT!

Negative Space

The goal of this activity is to see how you can creatively frame your subjects by using **negative space**. For this activity, you will use the sky, but for other pictures you can use anything with a solid color for the background.

WHAT YOU'LL NEED

>> An outdoor location during the day, with trees and/or buildings, where you can also see plenty of sky

Steps

1. For every subject you photograph, whether trees or buildings or anything else, you want to have the top half of your picture be only sky.
2. Try taking photos that have your subjects take up the bottom half of the image.
3. Then try taking photos that have your subjects take up only the bottom corner of your image.
4. Finally, take at least one picture where you make the subjects look very tiny at the bottom of the image.

📷 PHOTO TIP: Cropping

Cropping refers to cutting off a part of an image after the image is taken. You might crop an image because there is something in the image you do not want the viewer to see, or maybe you want to show a vertical perspective instead of a horizontal one. When experimenting with cropping, be careful not to cut out too much. If you do, the remaining image can look blurry on your screen or when you print it.

PHOTO LOG

How did including all the negative space in the image cause you to see your environment differently?

....

....

....

Of the pictures you took, which one did you like best and why?

....

....

....

CHAPTER THREE
Composition

Composition is how you arrange the elements, like the subject and background, inside your image, which angle you capture, and how close you are to the subject. Composition also refers to the shapes and lines in your image and how all the visual pieces work together. As you think about composition, look through the camera's viewfinder or at the screen of your smartphone before you take the picture. Look at each element in the frame. Does everything fit well together? Is there anything out of place, or that looks like it shouldn't be there? Make sure you not only look at your subject but also look at all four corners of your image. What would you change about the scene, if you could, to make all the elements in the scene work together visually? Consider what you can do: Change your perspective? Move your subject to make the composition better? Can you think of anything else?

You capture a *wide angle* when you zoom out and get more of the scene in front of you. You might consider taking a wide-angle photo when taking a picture of a beautiful land-scape. You capture **close-ups** when you zoom in and get less of the overall scene. You might consider a close-up angle when taking a picture of a bird or other animal from far away. And *medium angles* are between the other two. You might want to take a medium-angle shot if you are capturing a photo of a person in front of a beautiful background.

Are you looking at your subject at *eye level*, which means look-ing at it straight on? Or are you below your subject, looking up at it? Or are you above your subject, looking down at it? The answer will determine the angle of the photograph you take. Each angle gives a different feeling to an image. When you pho-tograph a person or object from below, you make the subject look bigger than it really is. When you photograph a person or object from above, you make the subject look smaller than it is.

Distance

What is your distance from your subject? Are you close to it or far away from it? Remember, this is different from zooming in and out. Distance is about being physically close or far away from the subject. Sometimes you must be far away, like when you are taking a picture of a tiger at a zoo. Sometimes you will need to be close, like when you take a picture of someone at a crowded birthday party (after asking permission!).

Space

Imagine you are photographing a friend and her dog on the beach. In your image, you can place your friend in between her dog and the water (with the dog closest to you), or you can place your friend closest to you, with the dog next, and the water farthest away. You can center your friend and her dog or position them to the right or to the left of the image. When you think about these things, you are thinking about how to use space.

Center or Off-Center

Pictures of people and objects usually show the person or object in the center of the image. The subject might be centered vertically, horizontally, or both. This makes sense, because, most of the time, things in the center of the image look great that way. Have you ever noticed that the most interesting images, though, have subjects off-center, which means the subject is not in the middle horizontally or vertically? You always have the choice to get creative with your images and have your subject be to one side of your image or in one of the corners!

Good Composition

Good composition is created when a photographer is thoughtful about the pictures they are capturing. One example of good composition is an image in which everything in it belongs in the image with no distracting elements. Great composition can include techniques that you will see in other places in this book, such as symmetry (see page 58). Another great compositional technique is to include diagonal lines in your image. Diagonal lines coming from one of the four corners (see page 104) of the image look particularly good.

Bad Composition

Bad composition, unfortunately, is much easier to achieve than good composition. One of the worst examples of bad composition is a portrait of someone taken when the photographer does not notice that the person has an object, such as a tree branch, behind them. Then it looks like the tree branch is coming out of their head! Another example of bad composition is an image that is almost symmetrical but not quite right—like when the subject of a picture is just slightly off-center. A cluttered background can also create a composition that will make a bad image.

PICTURE IT!

Composing Your Subject

If you are composing your subject, it means you are making all the creative decisions about the image. The goal of this activity is to have fun with how you compose your subject. You can expect your creative talents to expand while doing this activity!

>> 1 or more toys and/or a friend
>> An outdoor location with a variety of visuals (such as buildings, grass, or trees)

Steps

1. You can do this activity with a toy or a person, or you can do the activity once with a toy and once with a person.
2. Take 10 pictures of your subject or subjects. With each photo you take, change at least two things about the composition of the photo. You can change the background, your distance (how close or far away you are), how zoomed in you are, or the angle you use.
3. Your goal is to make 10 images that look like they were taken in different locations, each with a unique composition.

📷 PHOTO TIP: Props

Props are objects that you deliberately choose to include in a photo. We usually think of props as something used in portraits, but they can be used in any photo. You can use these objects to tell a story. They can hint at someone's personality or add a cool visual element.

PHOTO LOG

Was it easy or hard trying to create 10 pictures that look different from one another? Why do you think that is?

How did your pictures get better as you made changes, or did you like the first images you took best and why?

PICTURE IT!

Thinking about Space: Foreground, Middle Ground, and Background

The goal of this activity is for you to create an image in which a small object appears to be the same size as a large object. It is harder than it seems, but it makes for a very cool photo.

WHAT YOU'LL NEED

» A parent or other adult or a large object such as a tree

» A golf ball or something of similar size

Steps

1. Position yourself far away from the large object you have chosen.
2. Put the camera and the golf ball (or other small object) on the ground, close to each other.
3. Position the golf ball (or other small object) in the foreground (close to the camera) so it looks as big as the larger object you chose.
4. Lie on the ground so you are in position to take the photograph from down low.
5. You may need to take a few images and make adjustments to achieve the desired effect.

PHOTO TIP

It is easy to make a single person look bigger or smaller than they really are. If you are down low pointing your camera up at your subject, your subject will look bigger than they are in real life. The opposite is true: If you are up high and photograph the subject from above, they will look smaller.

PHOTO LOG

How many pictures did you need to take to create the intended effect?

....

....

....

Describe how moving the small object changed each photograph you took.

....

....

....

PICTURE IT!

Distance

The goal of this activity is to play around with how far away you are from your subject, which can make a big difference in what your final image looks like!

WHAT YOU'LL NEED

>> Something to throw, such as a plastic bracelet or a Hula-Hoop

>> An outdoor area with a lot of interesting things you might want to photograph (going to a park with a parent or other adult, if possible, will work well for this activity)

Steps

1. Pick a place to start.

2. From there, throw whatever object you have chosen away from you.

3. Go to wherever it landed.

4. From there, take a picture of something really close to you; for example, a blade of grass or a flower.

5. Repeat steps 2 through 4 at least 20 times, remembering to think about the various photo elements you have been learning, like framing. In each new location, take a picture of something a little farther away. By the time you finish, you will be taking pictures of things that are very far away.

PHOTO LOG

Look at your photos. How are they different from one another?

....

....

....

What do you notice about how the composition changed over time?

....

....

....

PICTURE IT!

Centered and Not Centered

The goal of this activity is to discover why centering your subject can be great and how much fun it is *not* to center your subject! Your creativity will expand with this activity.

WHAT YOU'LL NEED

» A walk around your neighborhood with a parent or other adult

Steps

1. Choose 10 different objects on your walk and take two pictures of each object. (You will end up with 20 different images.)

2. For each object, photograph it once with the object right in the middle of the image.

3. For the second image of the same object, photograph it off-center. You can put the object in the corner of the image, off to one side, or at the top or bottom of your image. This is your chance to get creative!

PHOTO LOG

Which images did you like better—those in which you centered your subject or the images in which you did not center your subject? Why do you think that is?

....

....

....

Name three creative choices you can make whenever you take pictures.

....

....

....

PICTURE IT!

Symmetry

The goal of this activity is to discover the magic of symmetry and why it works so well in photography. Symmetry occurs when the left and right sides of an image match. You will see symmetry all around you after this activity.

WHAT YOU'LL NEED

» At least 3 different rooms in your home

Steps

1. Walk around your home and look for pictures you can take where the left side of the image matches the right side, such as a bed with side tables on both sides or a table that has the chairs positioned on both sides.
2. Find 10 examples of symmetry in your home and capture them with your camera.
3. For some images, you might get really close to your subject. For some, stand farther away.
4. If you are having a hard time finding 10 scenes to photograph, go outside and do the same activity until you create 10 images.

📷 PHOTO TIP: Symmetry

Symmetry does not need to be exact. Imagine you take a picture of a stairway in which the railing on the left side exactly matches the railing on the right side, but there is a lamppost on only one side of the stairway. That is okay! Symmetry means "mostly equal." Using symmetry in composition is one of my favorite visual techniques because it really makes images interesting.

PHOTO LOG

Was it easy or hard to find symmetry in your home? What made it so?

....

....

....

List some ways you are starting to see your environment differently now that you are looking for great compositional techniques.

....

....

....

PICTURE IT!

Small Objects

When you take a picture of a mountain, you cannot move the mountain. But when you take pictures of small objects, you can move them all you want! Now you will practice composing your image by moving your subject around.

WHAT YOU'LL NEED

» Your favorite snack

» A plate or a bowl

» Your favorite drink

» A table

Steps

1. Put your favorite snack on the plate or into the bowl and place it on a table. Set your favorite drink next to it.

2. Find the best angle to photograph the food and drink you chose.

3. Choose the best background.

4. Move the snack and the drink around as many times as you need to get the best image.

5. If you have a flash, try photographing the snack with and without your flash. Decide which you like better.

PHOTO LOG

How many pictures did you take before you found one you really liked? What did you like about that particular picture?

_____

_____

_____

How is taking pictures of small objects different from taking pictures of large objects?

_____

_____

CHAPTER FOUR
Lighting

Now that you have framing and composition down, we are going to talk about lighting, which is particularly important in photography. If you do not have light, you cannot take a picture. Also, you can be creative with how you use lighting to create stunning images!

At the start of this book, we said that when you take a photograph, it is like you are painting with light. Every single image involves light of some kind. Without light, you cannot create a picture.

The word lighting refers to how your subject is lit. There are so many ways your subject can be lit. The most common source of light in images is the sun. Even when the day is cloudy and gloomy, the light outside is still the sun coming through the clouds. When you are inside, the lighting comes from whatever lights are turned on. Usually, you cannot move lights but you can if you have a table lamp nearby, for example. If you are taking a portrait, you can move your subject, so they are lit the way you want them to be. Start to notice the light for every image you create!

Indoor versus Outdoor Light

If you are inside your home with all the lights turned on, and then you go out the door into the sunlight, you might think the lighting in both places is similar. But take a closer look. Sunlight lights things in a particular way. In fact, the light in your neighborhood will look different at different times of the day. The light will look different when the sun is out and when the sun is covered by clouds. And all types of sunlight look different than the light that comes from the lamps and light fixtures in your home. See if you can notice the differences.

Soft Light versus Hard Light

Light comes in all different shapes and sizes! The sun is huge, far away, and very bright. A light bulb is small, a lot less bright, and sometimes positioned very close to your subject. A light bulb by itself is different from a light bulb inside a lamp. There is also cloudy light and light that we call shade, which is when sunlight is blocked by something. *Hard light* is what we call the light that results when there is nothing between the light source and your subject, such as a bare light bulb. *Soft light* is what we call the light that results when there is something between the light source and the subject, such as a lampshade or clouds.

Lighting Direction

Imagine you are taking a portrait of your favorite actor, singer, or musician. Imagine you have a photography studio with a lot of lights that you can move around. Where would you put the lights? Would you put one light shining directly on your subject's face? Would you have one light on the right and another light on the left? Would you put a light behind your subject, so they are lit from behind? Look at portraits you like and see if you can tell where the light was coming from when the picture was taken.

Natural Light

Most cameras have a flash. If you use **natural light** for your photographs, it means you do not use the flash. Instead, you use whatever light is already in the scene you are capturing, whether it is sunlight or light from indoor or outdoor lights. If you have a flash on your camera, you can always take one picture with a flash and one without to see which you like better. Use natural light to show exactly how a scene looked to your eyes when you took the picture. Use flash when you want more light on your subject.

Shadows

Shadows are dark areas in a scene where the light is blocked in some way. Shadows show up in practically all images, even if they are not the first thing to capture your eye. Shadows can be soft (meaning they are faint or transparent) or harsh (meaning they are heavy or dark). Usually, we think of an image with more shadows as being moodier. You can get creative with how you use shadows. If most of your image is shadows and only a small part of your subject is lit up, you will draw attention to the lit part of the image.

Using a Flash

Does your camera have a flash? If you are not sure, ask a parent or other adult to help you find out. The flash on your camera is bright, which is great, but it is also small, so you must be aware of how far the light from your flash can travel. If you are at a concert and you are far away from the stage, your flash will not make any difference, because you are too far away from your subject for the light to reach it. You typically have to be close to your subject for the light from your flash to reach it. The smaller your camera, the closer you will have to be.

PICTURE IT!

Using Natural Light

The goal of this activity is to get as many uniquely lit images as you can to see how you can use natural light to take great photos. You will learn how to use light in any scene you are photographing, whether you are indoors or outdoors.

WHAT YOU'LL NEED

>> A plate of colorful food (such as fruit, vegetables, or assorted cookies)

>> A 2-foot-square piece of sheer white fabric

Steps

1. Do this activity during the day and do not use your flash!

2. You'll put the plate in different lighting environments—if possible, try to get at least 20 shots.

3. Go outside and experiment with direct sunlight from above. Try your photographs in the shade as well.

4. Go back inside and take a picture with the plate near a window. Take a photo with the food near a lamp as well.

5. For each setup, take a second photo with the sheer fabric between the light and the plate to change the quality of the lighting.

PHOTO LOG

Which lighting setup did you like best and why?

....

....

....

How are you starting to notice the light in your environment in a new way?

....

....

....

PICTURE IT!

Photographing in Low Light

The goal of this activity is to become comfortable taking pictures in **low light**, which can sometimes be harder than taking pictures in brighter environments. You will learn how to be creative even when you do not have a lot of light available to you!

WHAT YOU'LL NEED

>> A lamp you can move

>> A parent or other adult

Steps

1. For this activity, do not use your flash!

2. Do this activity once it is dark outside in a safe location.

3. The lamp should be your only source of light. Turn off all other lights.

4. Take 15 portraits of the adult, moving the lamp or your subject around so the lighting is different in each picture.

5. Have your subject try to express a different emotion in each **pose**: happy, sad, excited, angry, confused, loving, surprised, etc. Use the light to accentuate the feeling on your subject's face.

PHOTO TIP: Using the Flash

Most, but not all, cameras have a built-in flash. A lot of people do not like using their flash because it can make images look washed out, which is when the subject looks much brighter than the background. If you get creative with it, however, the flash can be a fun tool to use. If you are finding that your flash is too bright, you can also simply move farther away from your subject.

PHOTO LOG

Which light setup did you like best and why?

....

....

....

Do you prefer photographing during the day or at night? Why?

....

....

....

PICTURE IT!

Composing with Shadows

Usually, when we look at a scene, our eyes focus on the parts of the scene that are lit up. The goal of this activity, however, is to learn how to creatively use shadows as a part of your images.

WHAT YOU'LL NEED

>> A sunny day

>> A parent or other adult (optional)

>> Trees, plants, or window shades that create interesting shadows

Steps

1. Your goal is to capture 10 different and interesting shadows in both indoor and outdoor pictures.

2. Feel free to move objects around in your environment. For example, you might ask an adult to lower the window shades in a sunny window to cast unusual shadows.

3. Get creative! Experiment with photographing in black and white. Choose any subject that seems interesting to you.

4. Remember to think before you snap the picture—and make adjustments before and after each one, if necessary.

PHOTO TIP

If you have two smartphones available to you, one way of playing around with light is to take a picture with one phone while you light your subject with the flashlight of the other phone. You can move the phone with the flashlight around to find the best way to light your subject.

PHOTO LOG

How are you starting to see shadows in a new way?

....

....

....

Describe how shadows can contribute to the look of your images in
a great way.

....

....

....

PICTURE IT!

Capturing a Rainy Day

When you look out the window and see that it is raining, you might think to yourself: *This is a bad day to take pictures*. Not necessarily! As long as you are careful not to get your camera wet, you can create a beautiful picture in the rain. The goal here is to capture rain and light in a new and inventive way.

WHAT YOU'LL NEED

>> A rainy day

>> A parent or other adult

>> 1 umbrella

>> 1 battery-powered strip of LED lights or a flashlight

>> Tape

Steps

1. Before going outside into the rain, tape the LED lights into the inside of the umbrella. If you do not have LED lights, hold a flashlight and point it into the umbrella.

2. Try all the various ways you can think of for how the lights and umbrella are set up.

3. Go outside and ask the adult helper to hold the umbrella. Take photographs of them with the LED lights turned on and off.

4. Remember, unless your camera is waterproof, you must always keep your camera dry. To do this activity, you can stand somewhere dry (like under an awning), stay inside and take the photo through a doorway or window, use a second umbrella, or even put a plastic sleeve over the camera.

5. Play with the placement of the umbrella to light your subject in different ways.

PHOTO LOG

Were you able to see the rain in your images? Was the rain visible in the entire image or only the rain that was lit up?

....

....

....

Which was your favorite image and why?

....

....

PICTURE IT!

Silhouettes

Have you ever seen a picture where the subject appears black with a brighter background behind the subject? This is called silhouette! The goal of this activity is to learn how to create silhouette images.

WHAT YOU'LL NEED

» A parent or other adult

» A doorway in your home between the inside and the outside

Steps

1. Do this activity during the day when the sun is out.

2. Have your adult helper stand in the doorway with the door open.

3. Stand inside your home and take a picture of your subject (adult helper) with the bright background behind them. You will notice that your subject, in the image, is dark.

4. Ask your subject to do some posing in the doorway to create fun shapes and take more photos.

PHOTO TIP

Most cameras allow you to adjust what is called the *exposure* (how dark or light you want an image to be) before you take a picture. Search online for how to adjust the exposure on your specific camera or smartphone if you want to experiment with this. This will be particularly helpful when you are doing the Silhouettes activity. When you do that exercise, if you want your pictures to be darker to create a better silhouette, use your exposure setting to make your image darker.

PHOTO LOG

You are becoming an expert at how to use light in your images! How do you look at light differently now from when you first started taking photographs?

....

....

....

Where else do you think you can create a silhouette?

....

....

....

PICTURE IT!

Window Light

Light from windows is one of the best kinds of light for portraits. The goal of this activity is to see how magical window light can be by taking selfies.

WHAT YOU'LL NEED

» A window

Steps

1. Do this activity on a day when the sun is out and you will be home all day.
2. Pick a window that has a lot of light coming through it.
3. Take a selfie at regular intervals during the day, as many as you can manage, such as at 10:00 a.m., 12:00 p.m., 2:00 p.m., 4:00 p.m., and 6:00 p.m. The times don't have to be exact, and you do not have to take a photograph at all the times listed. The point is to get pictures at regular intervals throughout the day and then compare how the different light makes each image different.

📷 PHOTO TIP: Motion

Motion can be hard to capture in a photograph. If you have pets who run around your home, you might find that all your images of them are blurry. You might be able to solve this problem by changing settings on your camera, but you can also try going to a place with lots of sunlight. More light in your scene makes it easier to capture frozen (not blurry) motion. At other times, you might want the motion in your image to be blurry. This can be a cool effect if you are taking pictures of someone running or playing, for example. It is easier to capture blurry motion with a regular camera, not a smartphone, in a darker environment. Try it!

PHOTO LOG

Do you like taking pictures of yourself? Why or why not?

_____

_____

_____

Pick your favorite picture. What time of day was it taken? Why do you like it better than the other pictures?

_____

_____

_____

CHAPTER FIVE

Depth and Dimension

Depth and dimension are two elements that work together to give a photo a sense of space. In this chapter, we will think about what this means and how it matters to your photos. Have you ever looked at an image and immediately imagined that you could walk into the scene that is depicted? Whenever you have this experience, it means the image has both depth and dimension to it. Images with depth look three-dimensional. Images that do not have depth look two-dimensional and flat. Depth can make the difference between the viewer being engaged with a photo and losing interest. Dimension refers to three parts of every scene in an image: the foreground (closest to the camera), the background (farthest away from the camera) and the middle ground (everything between the foreground and background). Images with dimension take advantage of all three spaces. Images with dimension are usually very interesting!

Shape

What are the **shapes** of the various elements in your image? Do you have squares and rectangles (like buildings), or circles and curves (like plates of food)? There might be lines that are straight or curved. There might be one large shape in your image that dominates the composition. You might have a lot of small shapes in your image that either make up a pattern or, perhaps, are more random. You can think of shapes as being two-dimensional whereas our next concept, **form**, is three-dimensional.

Form

When looking at an object in real life, you see it in three dimensions. In images, objects of every kind can sometimes look flat, but sometimes the light in a photograph can highlight the three-dimensional aspect of the objects. This is a wonderful visual effect to capture in your images. It can contribute to your image's depth. When you see pictures of objects for sale in advertisements, you will notice that the object is photographed in the best light, so the object in the image has form to it.

Framing to Add Perspective

As you learned earlier, perspective refers to where you are in relation to your subject. If you position yourself on the other side of an open door or open window from your subject, you can affect how the viewer of your images sees the scene. In this case, they will have two experiences of an image being "framed"—one frame is the border of the image, and the other is the internal border of the doorway or window in the image. This technique can give an image interesting layers.

Depth of Field

Have you ever seen an image of a flower or a person in which the subject is very sharp and in focus but the background is blurry? What you have seen in these images is something called a **shallow depth of field**. The **depth of field** describes how much of an image is in focus. A shallow depth of field means that, usually, only the subject is in focus. A **deep depth of field** means that everything in the scene is in focus. Pictures of nature landscapes, like mountains, usually have a deep depth of field so the viewer can see all parts of the image clearly!

PICTURE IT!

Using Light to Create Depth and Dimension

Outdoors, the light is always changing. If you go outside your home and sit and watch the light for an hour, the light will change during that time as the sun moves and clouds come and go. The goal of this activity is to see how you can use light, at different times of the day, to make your images pop.

WHAT YOU'LL NEED

» Alarm clock or timer

» Something stable to put your camera on, such as a tripod, a pile of books, or a piece of furniture

Steps

1. First thing in the morning, choose your favorite landscape around your home.

2. Set up your camera on a steady, sturdy surface. Take your first picture.

3. Set the timer for 1 hour.

4. When the timer sounds, put your camera in the same place and take the same picture.

5. Set the timer, again, for 1 hour and repeat step 3.

6. Keep taking a picture every hour for the entire day (or as long as you can).

📷 PHOTO TIP

To get some light streaks in your image, point your camera so the sun is just outside the border of your frame. You will see that if you position your camera just right, you will get beautiful light streaks that will make your image look stunning.

PHOTO LOG

Which image is your favorite and why? What time of day did you
take that image?

....

....

....

What do you notice the most about depth and dimension?

....

....

....

PICTURE IT!

Shape versus Form: Dimension Matters

The goal of this activity is to show you how, when you photograph objects from different angles, you can affect how those objects appear in your images! You will discover how to make your images pop, so the viewer will feel like they can reach out and touch the object in the picture!

WHAT YOU'LL NEED

» Parent or other adult

» Step stool

» 5 to 10 colorful items, like shoes, toys, or food items

Steps

1. Arrange your colorful items on a table or on the floor in a visually appealing way. Fit everything into a square.

2. Position a step stool so you can stand on it to take photos from an angle directly above the objects. Carefully stand on the stool (ask your adult helper to keep you steady, if needed) and take a photo of the objects.

3. Next, stack your objects in any way that you like. Photograph them from whatever perspective you want so you are happy with the images.

4. Can you see how the images you shot from above highlight the shape of your objects, while images from other angles highlight the form of your objects?

PHOTO LOG

Do you like the image better that you photographed from above or from another perspective? Why?

....

....

....

How would you describe the difference between shape and form?

....

....

....

PICTURE IT!

Framing to Add Perspective

The goal of this activity is to learn how to use something in your scene to create a frame inside the image, making it easy for your viewer to put themselves in your shoes and look at the scene from your perspective. This is one of the best ways to communicate a story through your images!

WHAT YOU'LL NEED

» A parent or other adult

» A place where you can photograph through a window or doorway

Steps

1. Create a story your adult helper can act out for you—maybe they are a princess or a character in a video game.

2. While they act, take pictures of them.

3. Try photographing your subject through a window or doorway.

4. Stand far enough away so that the frame (the window or the doorway) shows up in each of your images.

PHOTO TIP

When you photograph a scene through a door that is almost fully closed, you give the impression to the viewer that you are spying on someone. Try this technique if you want to tell a story that includes mystery and secrets.

PHOTO LOG

Did the frame improve your images? Why or why not?

....

....

....

What do you imagine a viewer of your images would think about the story being told in the images?

....

....

....

PICTURE IT!

Capturing Depth

The goal of this activity is to see depth in your images in a whole new way. You will also start to look at the scenes differently. Photographers do not see the world around them as flat and two-dimensional. You are really starting to think like a photographer, and this activity will expand that skill!

WHAT YOU'LL NEED

>> A parent, other adult, or friend

>> A long sidewalk or other long path with visible lines on each side

Steps

1. Find a long sidewalk or a long path with visible lines on each side—but avoid roads.

2. Have your helper stand at the end of the path, far away from you.

3. While they walk slowly toward you, take multiple pictures.

4. Include the entire path and your friend's face in each image.

PHOTO LOG

What do you notice about depth in each picture?

....

....

....

If you had to pick the best portrait, which one would you choose? Why?

....

....

....

PICTURE IT!

Capturing Dimension

The goal of this activity is for you to become more skilled at creating dimension in your images. You will be able to take advantage of all the parts of your scenes you are photographing: the foreground, the middle ground, and the background.

>> 2 colorful toys

>> A visually interesting outdoor area

Steps

1. Take 10 pictures that include both toys you've chosen. In each picture, put one of the toys close to you (about 3 feet away) and put the other toy farther away (about 10 feet away).

2. Imagine there is a story happening with each scene you create. If these two toys were characters in a movie, what would the story be about them? You can switch which toy is close to you and which is farther away to tell that story in your images!

PHOTO LOG

Which image was your favorite? Why?

....

....

What is the story you were trying to tell? Would someone looking at your images be able to guess the story correctly?

....

....

PICTURE IT!

Creating a Shallow Depth of Field

The goal of this activity is to learn how to create a photograph with the object in focus in front of a blurry background. This is a wonderful visual technique that brings all of the viewer's focus to the subject in your image!

WHAT YOU'LL NEED

>> A small object, such as a flower

>> An interesting background

Steps

1. Find a small object to photograph, such as a flower. Choose a background for your photograph that is far away from your subject, so there is a lot of distance between your subject and the background.

2. Position yourself about 2 feet away from your subject (the small object).

3. If you are using a smartphone camera, see if it has a portrait mode, which will work well. Set your camera to portrait mode, if available. If using a regular camera, you will want to zoom in on the object all the way.

4. Take at least five pictures like this. You can either take them of the same object or choose a new one for each image.

📷 PHOTO TIP

If you can zoom in and out on your camera, make sure to zoom in whenever you take a portrait—this will always make the person you are photographing look better. Step away and zoom in rather than stand close and zoom out.

PHOTO LOG

Is your eye drawn to the subject of your image because the background is blurry?

....

....

....

Do you like this visual technique? Why or why not?

....

....

....

CHAPTER SIX

Lines

Thinking about lines in photos—which direction they take, where they are placed, how they look with other things—can make for beautifully composed photos. Lines can sometimes be obvious in your images, like when you are taking a picture of a road with two yellow lines that are the brightest part of the image. Sometimes lines are more subtle, like when you have a line of trees in your landscape image. Each tree is its own line and there is also a line created by the row of trees. Using lines in images is a great way to create stunning photographs. Lines are fun for the eyes, if used properly, because they will lead your viewers' eyes from one place in the image to another! In this chapter, we will learn how to compose your images using lines.

Horizontal Lines

Horizontal lines go from side to side, across the image. Examples include the horizon, the top and bottom of windows, the top of the couch, and an electric wire stretching from your house or apartment to a pole outside. You will want to make sure that some strong horizontal lines in your images, like a horizon line, are exactly horizontal, which means they line up perfectly with the top and bottom of the image. If you take a picture at the beach and the horizon in your image is not perfectly horizontal, this can look "off" to your viewer.

To accomplish this, take just a moment before each snap to evaluate the lines, making sure the horizontal lines are exactly horizontal. Some cameras and smartphones have a grid you can turn on while you are photographing. This is a great way to make sure your horizontal lines will come out exactly horizontal.

Vertical Lines

Vertical lines run up and down. They can be created in many ways: by the two sides of a tall building, the lampposts on the side of a road, the left and right side of a doorway, or a flagpole. Sometimes, when you take pictures of tall buildings, the lines will not be perfectly vertical. This is called *distortion*. The only way to avoid distortion is to avoid taking the picture from ground level looking up, which changes the angle of the camera. Instead, you will need to take the picture from inside another nearby building so you are photographing the building straight on. Sometimes this is possible and sometimes it is not.

Diagonal Lines

Diagonal lines are straight lines that are not horizontal or vertical. These are my favorite lines, because they are interesting and playful. There is one kind of diagonal line that is particularly visually interesting in images: a diagonal line that starts at any of the four corners of your image. Imagine a picture of a field of flowers with a wooden fence on the left side of the field. The line of the fence starts in the lower left corner and goes from the foreground all the way into the background of the image. Can you imagine it? Can you see how that will create a wonderful, strong, visually interesting line in your image? This is a fun technique to try. Use diagonal lines to keep your images dynamic and attention-grabbing.

Curved Lines

Curved lines are not straight. Examples include the ivy growing in the park, the curve of a shell on the beach, the bending and intertwined branches of a tree, and the puffy cotton ball shape of the clouds in the sky. While straight lines lead the viewers' eyes from one place in the image to another, curved lines create a less direct path around an image, which can be fun. Imagine you are taking a picture of a beautiful park and, in your scene, there is a winding path leading into the background. Your viewers' eyes will follow that path all the way to the end.

Lines in Perspective

Lines in your image that highlight foreground and background are called **lines in perspective**. A picture of a long road leading into the background will have two lines that will guide the viewers' eyes to the background of the scene. In reality, the lines will be parallel to each other. In your image, they will always appear to be getting closer to each other the farther away they get. Sometimes these two lines go so far back into the background that it looks like they almost touch. This point, where they almost touch, is called the *vanishing point*!

Leading Lines

Leading lines guide your eye from one place in an image to another. In an image of a mountain, a path winding up the mountain will guide the viewers' eyes all around the image. In an image of the sand and ocean, the line where the water meets the sand will guide the viewers' eyes from one side of the image to the other or from the bottom of the image to the top. You might be noticing a theme with everything I have written about lines. They really do affect how your viewers see and experience your image!

PICTURE IT!

Vertical Lines

Remember, the goal of this book is to have you start thinking like a photographer. This means you will not only think about your images differently, but you will also start to look at your environments differently. The goal of this activity is to have you start to purposefully notice vertical lines all around you!

WHAT YOU'LL NEED

>> Trees! Lots of trees! If there are no trees around you, look for other vertical objects, such as ladders, lampposts, or a row of buildings along a sidewalk.

Steps

1. Take pictures of as many trees (or other vertical objects) as you can over the course of a day. Focus on trees with vertical trunks.
2. You can take pictures of one tree at a time, or you can find scenes with multiple trees.
3. If the weather is not great, it's also fun to work with vertical lines you see inside.
4. At the end of your photography session, choose your three favorite images.

PHOTO TIP: How Elements Interact

You can take great pictures by using one of the techniques in this book. This will highlight that particular technique. But you can also take multiple techniques and use them at the same time. For example, you might use a natural frame such as a window or door to frame your subject, and pair that with diagonal lines coming from the corner of your image. When you combine the techniques you have learned, you might create a dynamic and interesting image.

PHOTO LOG

Do you like including strong vertical lines in your images? Why or why not?

....

....

....

What do you like about the images you picked as your favorites?

....

....

....

PICTURE IT!

Horizontal Lines

Horizons are the farthest distance away that you can see. When you are at a beach, the horizon is where the water meets the sky. If you are in a large flat area, this is where the land meets the sky. The goal of this activity is to help you develop a whole new appreciation for horizontal lines just like you now have for vertical lines! This is good news, because photographers see lines around them all the time that they include in their images.

WHAT YOU'LL NEED

» Horizons! Lots of horizons!

Steps

1. Take as many pictures of horizons as you can in one day—if you can spread it out over a week, that is even better.

2. Some days you may not see any horizons and some days you may see a lot of them. Capture them in your photographs!

3. Before you take a picture, pause to think about the image you are about to create and make any adjustments to get the perfect image.

4. When you are done, choose your three favorite images. Try to take so many great photos that it is hard to pick your favorites.

PHOTO TIP

Another great visual element in pictures is patterns. Patterns are sometimes made up of repeating lines, but there are many kinds of patterns in the world. Any shape that repeats multiple times is a pattern. They are really fun to include in your images.

PHOTO LOG

Do you like vertical or horizontal lines better, or do you like them equally? Why?

....

....

....

What do you like about the images you picked as your favorites?

....

....

....

PICTURE IT!

Diagonal Lines

When I started to learn about photography, my favorite images were those with strong diagonal lines. I think they are the most dynamic part of any image! The goal of this activity is to get playful and discover how great diagonal lines can be.

WHAT YOU'LL NEED

» Objects with lines, like fences, walls, or buildings (outside), or a staircase, bed, or table (inside)

Steps

1. Remember, diagonal lines that come from the corner of an image are particularly appealing.
2. For this activity, take pictures in which you create diagonal lines that come from one of the four corners of your frame. Do this over the course of the week.
3. You can take all your images with your smartphone or camera horizontally or vertically, or you can play with tilting your smartphone or camera to create diagonal lines as well!
4. At the end of the week, choose your three favorite images.

PHOTO TIP

As a bonus activity, create images in which you have multiple diagonal lines coming from the various corners of your frame. First, try for two corners. Then try for three corners. Bonus points if you can take an image with diagonal lines coming from all four corners.

PHOTO LOG

What do you like about the images you picked as your favorites?

....

....

....

Among vertical, horizontal, and diagonal images, which is your favorite? Why?

....

....

....

PICTURE IT!

Curved Lines

The goal of this activity is to help you start to see all kinds of lines in your images. So far, you have had a lot of practice noticing straight lines, but now you will become skilled at noticing all the curved lines around you!

WHAT YOU'LL NEED

» A jump rope (or a playground)

» A parent or other adult

Steps

1. Hold one handle of the jump rope and ask your adult helper to hold the other end.

2. Take pictures of your helper while you move the jump rope between you, creating portraits with lots of curved lines in them.

3. You can also ask your helper to jump with the jump rope while you take pictures of them, capturing the curved line of the rope.

4. If you do not have a jump rope, ask an adult to take you to a playground instead. You can capture the curved lines on any play structure in the playground!

PHOTO LOG

Which do you like better: straight or curved lines? Why?

....

....

....

List all the places in which you notice curved lines now.

....

....

....

PICTURE IT!

Lines in Perspective

Now that you have done the activities with all kinds of lines, you will start to see how lines work together in images to create wonderful visual effects. The goal of this activity is to even further expand how you see lines. By the end of this exercise, you will be an expert in using lines in your images!

WHAT YOU'LL NEED

>> 1 set of dominoes or blocks

>> 1 table

Steps

1. Find a background you like for this image. It should be either a simple background with one color or a very colorful background.
2. On a table, line up the dominoes or blocks either in a straight row, or in a row that curves to the right or left.
3. Set the camera at the same level as the dominoes or blocks. If they are on a table, the camera should also be on the table.
4. Position your camera to capture the vertical lines in the image, then snap your picture.
5. It is okay to take a few photos to experiment with this setup.

PHOTO LOG

What do you notice about the lines in the images you created? Did the lines all work together to move your eye from the foreground of the image to the background of the image?

What are larger objects (like trees or buildings) that you can create the same effect with?

PICTURE IT!

Leading Lines

The goal of this activity is to put together all the activities you have done so far in this chapter! By the end of this exercise, you will be an expert at using lines in your images and will begin noticing them wherever you go!

WHAT YOU'LL NEED

>> A visually interesting indoor or outdoor environment with lots of lines

Steps

1. You want to get as many lines as possible in one image.

2. In each image, try to get horizontal, vertical, diagonal, and even curved lines, if you can. The more lines, the better!

3. Rather than having the image look chaotic, think through each image before you take the picture, so the image comes out pleasing to look at!

📷 PHOTO TIP: Backlighting

Backlighting is a technique where you put a strong light behind your subject or move your subject between you and the bright light source. Backlighting is often used for making portraits, like silhouettes (see page 78), but you can use it for any subject. The light creates a glow around the subject. You can do this with a bright lamp in your home, a flashlight, or any light you can find. You can also do this with the sun, as long as you don't look directly at it. Position your subject so it is between you and the light, then take the picture. You may need to practice this a bit before you get an image you really like, but the result is worth it.

PHOTO LOG

How have you noticed yourself getting more creative with lines in your images?

....

....

....

Of all the techniques in this book, what has been your favorite? Why?

....

....

....

You're a Photographer!

Congratulations! It is extraordinary that you have completed all the activities in this book. You can now go out in the world and honestly say you are a photographer. The magic of photography is that even though you have grown immensely through completing these activities, this might be just the beginning of a lifelong journey of telling stories through photography.

I am thrilled to see what you will be creating a month from now, a year from now, five years from now, even 10 years from now. Photography might be your way to connect with people, or to see other parts of the world, or maybe even make a difference in the world. In fact, I suspect that some of you reading this book will become professional photographers when you grow up. And for those of you who do, you will be part of a global creative community.

Whether you take pictures as a hobby or aspire to do it professionally, there is one secret to photography that I have waited this whole book to share with you. The *most important* element of taking pictures is to always, always, always have fun!

Glossary

angle: the position—above, below, or eye level—from which the photographer views the subject

aperture: the opening in a lens that gets smaller or bigger

background: whatever is behind your subject

backlighting: a lighting technique for which you place a strong light source behind the subject

camera body: on a standard camera, the main and biggest part of the camera, not including the lens

candid: an unposed image taken while the subject is not paying attention to the camera

composition: how you choose to place the elements in your frame

contrast: the amount of difference between the lightest and darkest areas of an image

cropping: cutting off parts of the image after you have taken it

curved lines: lines that are not straight

deep depth of field: when everything in a scene is in focus so the viewer sees all parts of the image clearly

depth: the quality of sensing the distance between objects in an image

depth of field: describes how much of an image is in focus

diagonal lines: straight lines that are not vertical or horizontal

dimension: interesting elements in the foreground, middle ground, and background of your photo

edit: to alter an image after it has been taken, often using a computer program or an app on a smartphone

exposure: how bright or dark an image is

focus: refers to the objects in a photo that are clear instead of blurry

foreground: whatever is closest to the camera in your image

form: the quality of an object in an image that looks three-dimensional

framing: the artistic choices you make about how you create the borders of your image in relation to the elements in your image

horizontal lines: straight lines that go from side to side in an image

image sensor: inside digital cameras, a flat rectangular piece of hardware that can read light and turn that light into a digital image file

ISO rating: the ISO rating indicates the sensitivity of the camera to whatever light is coming into it

leading lines: lines in an image that guide the viewers' eyes from one part of a scene to another

lens: the cylinder on the front of the camera; on some cameras, you can replace the lens with another lens

lighting: refers to how your subject is lit

lines: can guide the viewers' eyes from one part of an image to another; can be straight and horizontal (going from left to right), straight and vertical (going from top to bottom), straight and diagonal (going from one corner to another), or curved

lines in perspective: lines in your image that highlight foreground and background

low light: conditions for photographing that do not have a lot of light, like evenings, or when you are indoors

middle ground: the area between the foreground and background in a photo

natural light: the light used to take pictures without using a flash

negative space: empty area in an image, which might be sky or a single-color wall

perspective: the vantage point from which a photograph is taken

pixels: the tiny squares of color that make up a picture (these squares are so tiny you usually cannot see them)

pose: to stand, sit, or lie in a deliberate way

shadows: dark areas in a photo where the light in the scene is blocked in some way

shallow depth of field: when only the subject of the photograph is in focus

shapes: the contour or outline of the various objects in an image

shutter speed: the length of time light is let into a camera when a picture is taken

silhouette: an image in which the subject is so dark that only its shape is visible

staging: deliberate placement of objects in a scene

subject: the most important element in an image

vertical lines: straight lines that go up and down in an image

viewfinder: the opening you look through to see the scene you are about to photograph before taking the picture; not all cameras have one

zoom: a camera function that, when changed, makes it look like you are closer to or farther from your subject, and allows you to include more or less of the scene you are photographing; some lenses can zoom and others cannot

Resources

100cameras. The Where You Are Workshop, 100cameras.org/wya.

Bidner, Jenni. *The Kids' Guide to Digital Photography: How to Shoot, Save, Play with & Print Your Digital Photos.* New York: Sterling, 2011.

Ebert, Michael, and Sandra Abend. *Photography for Kids! A Fun Guide to Digital Photography.* Sebastopol, CA: O'Reilly Media, 2011.

Glassel, Philip R. *Photography for Kids (and Novices of All Ages): Beginning at the Beginning.* Las Vegas, NV: CreateSpace Independent Publishing Platform, 2013.

Honovich, Nancy, and Annie Griffiths. *National Geographic Kids Guide to Photography: Tips & Tricks on How to Be a Great Photographer from the Pros & Your Pals at My Shot.* Washington, DC: National Geographic Children's Books, 2015.

Jacquart, Anne-Laure. *Photo Adventures for Kids: Solving the Mysteries of Taking Great Photos.* San Rafael, CA: Rocky Nook, 2016.

Meyerowitz, Joel. *Seeing Things: A Kid's Guide to Looking at Photographs*. New York: Aperture, 2016.

Proujansky, Alice. *Go Photo! An Activity Book for Kids*. New York: Aperture, 2016.

Sharp Shots Photo Club YouTube channel. YouTube.com /channel/UCHrcw3R1oP7obqIrsA712Jw.

Acknowledgments

Thank you to anyone I have ever taught photography to. I was only able to write this book because of you. Thank you, Angela, for living a life dedicated to amplifying kids' stories and for giving me the opportunity to teach. Thank you, Launa, for seeing the leader in me before I saw it in myself. Thank you, Rudy, for teaching me that hospitality and family are often the same thing. Thank you to my family for having so many kids so that, by the time I started teaching, talking to kids was second nature. Thank you, Indigo, my muse, for putting the lily on your table in Florence so I could take a picture of it and realize that I love photography. Thank you, Dylan and Erin. If Vincent and I are ever trapped on a deserted island, we're choosing you to be stuck with. Thank you, Mom, for giving me the gift of finding the adventure and fun in everything I do. Thank you, Dad, for giving me your fighting spirit, which I get to use to make a difference in the world. Thank you, Amber. I wrote this book for me at 12 and you at 9 and imagined us doing the activities in this book together. Thank you, Adam, for teaching me to never take things too seriously. Thank you, Becky, for loving my sense of humor. Thank you, Neil, for your gentle grace and, most of all, for the cupcakes and donuts. Thank you, Lydia, for causing my leadership, holding me accountable and, most of all, for the dance parties. Thank you, Vincent, for laughing at my jokes sometimes but not other times, and when you don't laugh, I can't stop laughing, and being with you is truly my happy place.

About the Author

JP Pullos started taking pictures professionally in 2006. His images have been published in the *New York Times, GQ,* and other publications, and his work has been exhibited in New York City galleries. In 2011, JP founded JP Teaches Photo (jpteachesphoto.com), a company that has sold more than 80,000 photography classes to photography enthusiasts in 165 countries in the world. JP is also the Photography Education Coordinator for 100cameras (100cameras.org), a nonprofit organization that works with kids around the world who have had challenging experiences and teaches them how to process and tell their stories through photography. JP lives in New York City with his husband, Vincent.

Printed in the USA
CPSIA information can be obtained
at www.ICGtesting.com
LVHW060102040124
767690LV00001B/1